Prophetic Dance

Lynn M Hayden

Prophetic Dance

Lynn M Hayden

FIRST EDITION 2003

Second Printing December 2005

Third Printing January 2009

ISBN: 0-9771925-4-7

Copyright © 2003, Lynn M. Hayden

Dancing For Him Ministries, Inc.

All rights are reserved. This book is protected under the copyright laws of the United States of America. This reference guide may not be reprinted or copied for commercial gain or profit. The use of short quotations or occasional page copying for personal or group study is permitted and encouraged. No permission is necessary for that.

Book Design Jessica Mitchem
Production SPS Publications Eustis, Florida
www.spsbooks.com

Other books by the author

Dancing For Him

Dance, Dance, Dance!

Team Terrificus

Processionals, Props, & Pageantry

Divine Choreography

Dance In The Church, What's The Pointe?

Creative Worship

Handwritten notes:

I will change you focus

Here to bring healing to your soul
When you don't understand my hand trust my heart
I am so close to you
Fit for a king

Awaken Passion in my people
I'm a waker passion

Table of Contents

Introduction. 9
Demystification 13
See, Hear, Feel 17
Musical Word 29
On The Spot. 37
Pre-Planned?. 47
Power of Praise 55
Healed!. 63
Conclusion. 73
Music Suggestions. 74

Introduction

Through exercises, that are designed to teach people how to hear the Father's heart (and express it prophetically through word, song, & dance), this book describes, primarily, the demystification of prophetic dance. Though not exhaustive, this simple, introductory approach will ease curious minds and shed some ambient light on the subject.

The workbook type layout, is planned so a worshipper, worship dancer, or leader (who is interested in either being activated themselves, or leading others into a deeper understanding of prophetic movement) may incorporate this myriad of exercises, intended to "activate" and stir up their resident gift of prophesy.

Basically, this training will stimulate creativity and cultivate comfort in the execution of prophetic dance.

Some of the exercises include:
- Ministering to individuals
- Working in pairs
- Prophesying to a congregation
- Ministering through movement
- Interpretive movement during a prophetic word or song.
- Working as a group.

Years ago, when I first heard the word "activation," I really didn't know what in the world it meant. During a prophetic training seminar, I had done some exercises that were fun, and just assumed that they had imparted activation to me. So like a good leader/follower, I decided to do likewise. In one of our conferences (a long time ago), I prayed for everyone to receive activation. Although not totally wrong, what I didn't realize was that activation only meant to stir up the gift that is within you (or make it active). This is done through learning as you practice; in other words, learning by doing.

Throughout this book, I'll give you exercises that have been and could be done in a workshop setting or dance team practice time. The produced results will be: ease in ministry dance; a greater aptitude to hear God's heart; and a self confidence to express it freely.

It is my hope and desire that you will not only be better equipped to minister for God (by expressing His heart), but also will have such a clear understanding of what to do, that Prophetic Dance will no longer be a mystery, but a rewarding joy.

Chapter One
DEMYSTIFICATION

Webster's definition of prophecy is: "Prediction of the future under the influence of divine guidance; something prophesied or predicted; divinely inspired utterance or utterances of a prophet."[3]

First, let us take a look at prophesy, with the purpose of demystification. Many people look at prophesy as spooky, or mystical. However, to make it plain and simple, it is just *hearing and expressing God's heart*. How do we hear God? He speaks to us several ways, so let's take a look at a couple of examples.

"I have spoken by the prophets, and have multiplied visions; I have given symbols through the witness of the prophets." (Hosea 12:10)

The most simple to understand and usually the first way, is through the Bible (the Word of God). These are God's words, given to us by the prophets, that contain instruction, promises, and warnings. They tell of His love for us, about His character, and His brief historical biography.

This form of communication between God and man is very reliable and totally true. In the scripture above, "through the witness" literally means by the hand of the prophets. Could this be the hand writing or written account of what God said?

He also says that He has multiplied visions. There are accounts in the Bible where people have had visions. They then get the interpretation and take it as practical instruction for their lives or others'.

"Vision—chazon: Strong's #2377: A prophetic vision, dream, oracle, revelation; especially the kind of revelation that comes through sight, namely a vision from God. This noun occurs 35 times and is from the root chazah, "to see, behold, and perceive." Chazon is especially used for the revelation which the prophets received. The prophets understood God's counsels so clearly because He revealed matters to them by visible means. Proverbs 29:18 shows that when a society lacks any revelation from God (divine insight), such a society heads in the direction of anarchy."[2]

We too are able to receive visions. This is a wonderful way to hear from God. I am a very visual person and have seen many visions over the years, but never knew what to do with them or what they meant until someone told me how (I'll explain more later).

Finally, we can hear from God through symbols. These are literally parables. We know, by reading the gospels that Jesus often used parables to communicate. These are basically stories to give us a verbal and visual understanding of a subject. In a simple nutshell, so to speak, prophetic dance is essentially: either interpreting God's word directly from the bible, from hearing His voice, or receiving a vision from Him and then acting it out through movement. This action enhances the onlooker's understanding of the message that is coming from the throne room of God. Prophetic messages from God, will guide, instruct, bring forth healing, deliverance, and change to set the imprisoned free!

Chapter Two
SEE, HEAR, FEEL

Habakkuk 3:6—*"He stood and measured the earth; He looked and startled the nations and the everlasting mountains were scattered. The perpetual hills bowed. His **ways** are everlasting."²*

Ways—Halijkah—walking, or marching in procession; move as in a caravan.

There is power in movement. God looked and startled the nations. Not only were the mountains scattered, but hills even bowed. His ways are everlasting. God's movements are so powerful (when He moves in a procession) that even the mountains respond to His glance. How powerful against the enemy is our movement when the all powerful God is resident within us?! Other references: Ps. 68:24, Proverbs 31:27 (the goings or ways).

Do we not speak with our bodies through the dancer's language of movement? We can tell a story with our bodies even if there is no music at all. As Spirit filled believers, our bodies can speak divinely inspired utterances. We can call those things into existence that be not as though they were.

Even as someone with the gift of prophecy can hear from God about an individual or situation and deliver it through word or song, so can a dancer with the gift of prophecy hear from God and deliver a message through movement. There are several ways through which this can be accomplished. These will be discussed throughout the book.

The following is an excerpt from my Dancing For Him book (referenced from several years ago). However, for clarity's sake, it bears repetition. Probably, the most pure form of prophetic dance is when the minister expresses the heart of God, through dance, by interpreting, (acting out or dancing out) a vision, word, or impression given by the Lord. I have done this many times, but the clearest example that I'd like to share, is when I was called upon (without any preparation or notice) to interpret what the Lord would say through the music that was about to be played prophetically. Talk about being stretched... The leaders said they had never done this before and I was the one who was called upon to act on faith and present the interpretation. I hesitantly walked up on the huge, empty stage, and said "Lord, help."

The minute the prophetic anointing was released, the Lord was faithful to show me a vision. The whole stage had turned into a furrowed field into which I was to plant seeds. Just like when we receive a prophetic word or vision, from the Lord and He only initially gives a small portion of it, if we are faithful to bring it forth, He is faithful to give us the rest. I acted on faith, and began to dance out the vision and plant the seeds. It was then, that the Lord gave me more. I began to make motions as if I were watering the plants, and motioned for the sun to shine on each one (there were four). Once the indication was made that they had grown enough to be sent out (as if to evangelize) by the wind of the Spirit, they were to later bring in a harvest themselves.

The worship leader then interpreted in song exactly what I had just demonstrated in dance. Then, the musicians and I went back and forth to the point where neither one knew who was interpreting whom. At times, it sounded like the music was following my lead or interpreting the dance, and at other times, I was interpreting the music. It was a beautiful demonstration of symbiotic harmony.

Since that experience, the Lord has stretched me (many times) even further. Another example was when we were in a store front church in Chicago. The young keyboard player did not have professional music training, but could play well enough to carry the worship time. The important thing was that this boy was anointed! The moment he touched the keyboard, the presence of God was powerfully evident. Because this prophetic anointing was so strong, it ignited something inside of me like I had never experienced before. I could actually hear God giving me the dancing instructions that would bring freedom to the people. First He said to play in the river, as if to splash around. When I did, there was such an overcoming joy that it could not be contained. Among other things, He told me to scoop up some of the water and splash the people! When I did, the whole half of the congregation kind of blew backwards, as if they had been drenched. Then He said to splash the other side of the church. They had the same reaction. Finally, He said go on the platform and splash the Pastors. Though it only seemed like a blink of an eye, I did not realize that I had been dancing for several hours! Everyone was blessed and the anointing was so strong, that no one wanted to leave. It is because of these type of experiences that I am so compelled to impart it to others.

Therefore, since I had experienced getting an impression, vision, or word, many times, it was then my turn to stretch others. I began teaching a very small portion of prophetic dance during workshops. I used to think, "let's just save this prophetic dance segment until the last half hour of the workshop and if we don't get to it—oh well!" The good problem was, that since there were such dramatic ministry results, the time slots expanded. People were consistently going through deliverance and experiencing deep inner healing, during those short workshop intervals. Now, I can't wait until that segment and usually allow an hour to an hour and a half to give people an opportunity to fully experience the anointing.

As I began teaching prophetic dance more prolifically, people wanted to know how to see, hear, or feel? Years ago, I used to think, "I'll never be able to prophesy like those seasoned prophets…" However, the Lord encouraged me through wonderful mentors. Being in the environment of a prophetic anointing helped, too. So I asked the Lord to help me and I began to practice.

I had been getting visions when I prayed, anyway, but didn't quite know what they were or what to do with them. By God's design, I was blessed to have the most precious fifteen minutes of private teaching time with a famous prophetess from England, and she enlightened me as to how to "prophesy the vision." She told me how to say what I saw, so others may be blessed, by simply describing what I saw, in fashion that would be clear to the hearer, almost like telling a story, and trust Holy Spirit to fill in the blanks. It seemed so easy when she described it, but I was still VERY cautious, as I really wanted to be sure I was hearing from God. My eyes were then opened.

I was also blessed to be able visit a strong prophetic training church, where I taught various forms of dance for a number of years (during their arts conferences). It was there that I got more intense training by observation, being in the environment, and being under their prophetic mantel. I learned many of the "activation" (learn by doing) exercises for prophesy there. Then the Lord showed me how to turn them into movement or dance.

It is not to say that everyone needs this kind of exposure to hear from God, though it has certainly helped. A strong relationship with the Almighty should be sufficient.

The following exercises and directions are what I usually do, during a workshop, to activate worshippers into prophetic dance. I usually begin by giving a brief explanation and preparation. So people are more relaxed, I basically say that prophetic dance is simply expressing the Father's heart. In other words, what does our Heavenly Father want to say to an individual or group in this day and hour? Then we start a series of practice exercises.

Ministering to Individuals

Beginning with ministering to individuals, break up into pairs. This is a good one to "break the ice," so to speak.

Each person, in the pair, ask their partner for permission to minister to each other. Once they have agreement, they close their eyes and pray in the spirit. Encourage them that those who don't have their prayer language to simply pray with their understanding.

After a short period they should go silent and LISTEN to hear God's voice, or LOOK to see a vision, or FEEL to sense an impression for that other person.

Once they have obtained something special from the Lord, they should (one at a time) dance out through simple interpretive movement, what they heard, saw, or felt. When one person is finished, and with out talking, the other one then should begin to interpret what they received from the Lord (for their partner).

Once both partners have finished "dancing it out," they then whisper to the other one about what they meant by their interpretation. It is important to whisper, so they do not disturb the others, in the room, who are still receiving ministry.

This same exercise may be done through song, where the partners sing their prophesies (with or without music).

It is amazing to see the immediate ministry results, even in the very first exercise. Though, often, people will have never done anything like this, God is faithful to touch their hearts.

Another exercise for individuals, where EVERYONE gets blessed, is what I call the "Final Blessing." The only reason I coined that term is because it was the last exercise and a positive way to end a complete day of intense, ministry workshop training. With upbeat music in the background and the knowledge that everyone would get a word from the Lord, the excitement built and people always went home blessed.

Start by placing people in single-file lines. The amount of time left for the exercise, should determine how many lines to create. Have all the people facing the front of the room. Then, have the lead person in each line turn around and face their respective lines.

The exercise is for the first person in the line to go up to the lead person (who just turned to face their line) and bless them with a one, two, or three phrase expression of edification, exhortation, or comfort. If it is called a blessing, then people are not so intimidated about giving them a "prophesy."

They are not to lay hands on the person, stay there to pray for the person, talk to the person, stand there and think of something, or say a long prophesy to them. They simply go up to them, say those quick couple words of encouragement and run to the end of the line (Example: prosperity; new levels; breakthrough; healing; expansion; new doors, etc.). While they speak their phrase, they motion with an interpretive movement, again, keeping everything very simple and to the point.

The purpose for not taking time to "think about it" is so that they get used to allowing God to work in them, through bypassing the intellect and working or speaking by faith.

The next person in line, then goes up to the leader and does the same thing. Once that person is finished, they, too go to the end of the line. Each person remaining in the line, also does the same thing.

Once everyone has had a turn, the blessed leader, also goes to the end of the line so they may be a blessing. The next person in the remaining line, then becomes the leader, who becomes blessed.

This whole cyclical process continues until the entire line has received ministry. Once a line is finished, then they stand and clap to the music to indicate to the facilitator that they are through.

Usually, when all the lines are finished. Everyone dances a "follow-the-leader-rumba-type" dance around the room. With a shout of praise, the meeting adjourns.

Sometimes, there are young people (both chronologically and spiritually) in the room, so it is good to comfort them. This all may be VERY new for a lot of people, so to make them feel more relaxed, tell them to bless their partner (if they didn't *see, hear, or feel* anything from God- which is rare). Giving the other one edification, exhortation, or comfort is all good, even if it is done by faith. This way, everyone feels like they are included.

Remember, that because this is a training environment and totally experimental, make sure no one prophesies babies, geographical moves, or marriage. This should be left up to seasoned prophets.

Also, it is a good idea to set a couple of guidelines like: don't go back to your hotel rooms or the parking lot to experiment with prophesy (unsupervised). This could cause much difficulty for the recipient and the hosting ministry. Imagine if one of your friends pulled you aside in the parking lot and gave you a "parking lot prophesy." If it were way off, it could send that person on a grueling path of confusion or despair. Not to mention the fact that the person who received this "bad advice" could tell others, "oh, I received this prophesy during such and such meeting at thus and so's ministry or dance team practice time." Ouch!

Also, aside from pure experimentation, in a supervised setting, if you happen to receive a prophetic word that has been tape recorded, be sure to write it out and bring it to your Pastor or overseer. This is so they may pray about it and give you wise counsel.

Whether you see visions, feel God through impressions, or actually hear His voice, they are all wonderful ways to minister the heart of God to individuals. One of the responsibilities of a worship leader is to express the heart of man to the heart of God as well as express the heart of God to the heart of man, through music. Likewise, a prophetic dancer's impetus is to not only express the heart of man to God, through worship, but also to express the heart of God to the heart of man, through their creative language of movement, thereby becoming a live instrument of worship and ministry.

I smelled the fragence of God

Chapter Three
MUSICAL WORD

Another form of prophetic dance is movement, done under the anointing, to music that is given divinely to a musician (or group of musicians), after which there is an interpretation through song (or word). A classic example of this is when I was at a meeting where I was given liberty to dance (always check with those in authority first). During the highly anointed praise and worship, an extremely gifted violin player began to play prophetically. Immediately, I saw a vision and got words to the prophetic song that would be an interpretation. I also saw a dance as a visual interpretation. My heart was pounding, indicating to me that I was to go up on the stage and interpret.

A bit of fear set in as I heard someone from the platform say something to the effect of "any activity bringing attention to itself, is a distraction." Goodness, how do you get past that when you know that God is nudging you forward? I heard the Lord say go, but I hesitated.

Then the woman who played the violin began to sing the interpretation, and it was *exactly* what the Lord had shown me. So, I bolted up on the stage and began to dance what I saw.

Once I got up on the stage, the basic theme of the prophetic word changed from what we had both initially heard, but I was still able to interpret very easily. I thought it rather strange that it all changed once I got up on the stage, but I believe God wanted my obedience, and He simply proved to me that I really did hear from Him, and just used that as a way to get me up there. Of course, the message probably meant a lot of things to a lot of people, but for me, it was a lesson of obedience, as well as reassurance, and God got all the glory.

Similar to the "See, Hear, Sense" exercises, in the previous chapter, so it is with interpreting music. It is a wonderful experience to dance to prophetic music. Sometimes, you just 'know' what God is saying, through the music. Sometimes, you just step out, by faith and God shows you as you go. Either way, it is ministry.

Keep in mind that prophetic music is something that comes from the throne of God and is a message, word, love song, or encouragement, etc. FROM God to the people. Don't be afraid to look your audience in the eye. If it were a worship song TO God, then our general focus would be toward Him (at least where you portray Him to be). On the other hand, however, songs or music that come from Him TO the people, should have directed focus toward the people to whom you are ministering.

The following is an example of what you might hear, see, or sense the Lord saying (through the instrumental music).

"Don't give up. I haven't brought you this far to forget about you or let you down. Though it seems like everything around you is faltering, just know that I will never falter. I will never leave you or forsake you.

I have seen your efforts and know your many trials. I have seen you try to put the dances together for Me. I have seen you try to put the teams together for Me. I have seen you try to get just the right costumes and props for Me. I have also seen you dancing in the back of the church, dancing down the aisles, and have cherished your dancing with Me. Do not lose heart. For not only am I with you, but I will raise you up and send you forth. Be persistent even in the fluctuations of your dance ministry (with people coming and going). Follow Me. Stay with Me and hear My voice of instruction. For I will lead you by the still waters and I will lay you down in green pastures. For I am yours and you are mine. You are not too old and it is not over yet. Your time and season is about to change. Walk with Me into your season."

He may give you something like this right on the spot, as the music is playing, or maybe while the music has been playing for a bit, you may sense something and interpret afterward. When you interpret these kinds of words, it is almost like using sign language or mime. The movements must be distinguishable and easy to understand or "read." Particularly when there are no words, sung by a singer, to help the recipient know what is being said. Sometimes, I will speak the word as I'm interpreting, especially if it is at close range, to an individual. If you are way far away, on the platform and there is a general word for the whole body, then the interpretations have to be crystal clear! Otherwise (although there is nothing really wrong with dancing to the music), all the congregation will see are some graceful gestures. This ends up being a form of performance with out any ministry. It is, of course, God's yearning to set us free and He will use whatever medium He can (dance, mime, music, song, etc.) to get the desired result.

I have found that since everyone is in the 'same boat', during a workshop or team practice, then they are very supportive of and encouraging to one another. No one wants to be wrong, when it comes to speaking (through dance, song, or word) for the Almighty, Creator of the Universe, All Powerful, Wonderful God! Keep in mind, however, that this is just PRACTICE. He is gracious, loving, and forgiving. He understands that we are making every effort to please and minister for Him. Be at ease and try.

It is funny, but there have been times when I've demonstrated an example of what prophesy should look or sound like (by just making something up), it ended up being from God and people received tremendous ministry. This proved to me that by being relaxed and not straining to hear, that He works through our yielded vessel (if we are just willing).

The following few exercises are designed to get people used to ministering God's heart with only instrumental music and no words. Please refer to the page, in the back of this book, for a list of some recommended prophetic music and resources.

Ministering With Music

Sometimes, it is easier to begin working with only one person (pairing up with a partner), then to feel intimidated by a small group or doing it solo in front of the whole, large group. You could start with the same exercise you did in the previous chapter, only this time use instrumental music (either live or recorded). Simply pray together, listen to the music, and take turns interpreting.

Secondly, get in groups of three or four and have one person at a time take turns listening to the music and ministering interpretively to those remaining in the group.

Once everyone has gotten a turn interpreting the music, then take it a step further. Even though this is the chapter about music, we're going to take it to the next level here, for a moment. With a group of three or four, have one person be the singer (or speaker), one person be the dance interpreter, and the other one or two be the receiving congregation. As the music plays, the singer sings or says what they sense God is saying, while the dancer ministers to the remaining congregation. This exercise is sometimes more of a stretch for the singer then the dancer. Let each person in the group have a turn at each station, either singing, being a good receiver, or enacting.

This exercise could go two ways. One is where the dancer could minister as if it were a word to the whole body of Christ (outward to a congregation). The other is where the dancer would go directly to one individual at a time. Often, I will do either (sometimes both), during a prophetic song. When I minister during a conference or while visiting a church, I typically start on the platform and do a general word/dance, then work my way through the audience where the Lord shows me individuals to whom I should minister. I will dance right in front of a particular person and occasionally touch them on the shoulder. On rare occasions, as Holy

Spirit leads, I will pause to pray for that person. The ministerial results always amaze me, as tears and anointing flow. Just for a word of advice or caution, here, though: if you are in the experimental stages and are not in leadership at your church, please be sure to check with those in authority over you, before attempting this level of ministry. We allow and encourage this in a closed, practice, safe environment of a workshop, but when it comes to actual ministry in your church, be sure you are submitted to authority and get permission. It would be a good idea to practice this during your dance team rehearsal times with the oversight of a seasoned dance minister or overseer.

Finally, during this segment of the workshop, I ask if there are any brave souls who would like to interpret the music by themselves. There is always at least one or two. Afterwards, sometimes, we either guess or they will tell us what their interpretation meant.

For a group, who either has had prophetic dance experience or feels very comfortable, we may all take turns interpreting short segments of the music. Kind of like a cyclical affect, everyone would line up on the floor in straight rows, in front of the stage or stage area. Then, one at a time (starting at one end of the line), each person takes a couple of moments to face the people and interpret. Either a monitor or the leader says, "next," at which time the next person goes up and the other one goes to the end of the row. Repeat this over until everyone has gotten a turn. It certainly breaks through that barrier of fear and is a lot of fun.

Even as David's harp brought deliverance and solace to a king, so can prophetic music minister God's heart to the people of today and bring forth His glorious freedom and peace.

All that He has for us is in the heavenly realm. We only need to be willing open vessels for His power and presence to flow. These exercises, will help prepare us to be those vessels, ready in season and out of season, so His purposes will be fulfilled in the earth realm. God's power is so intense, that when it touches our human heart, we become radically different. As we become visually manifested representations of the voice of the Lord, interpretive dance movements, done to prophetic music, can be the vehicle through which people will receive His power and be transformed forever.

Chapter Four
ON THE SPOT

A more common form of prophetic dance is when a prophetic song or word is directly coming forth and the dancer simply interprets the words, through dance, on the spot. I've done this many times, and people always say that through it, the Lord really ministered to their hearts. That's what it's all about anyway. We are not just dancers, but ministers of the gospel of Jesus Christ. One phrase I heard years ago was, 'it is easier to teach a minister to dance, then it is to teach a dancer to minister'. However, we need to be ready in season and out of season, to be called upon for ministry.

Just recently, I was visiting some friends out of state and for me that was only an hour and a half away. I originally was going to visit for dinner, then was invited to stay over night, so I would not have to drive back late at night. I agreed and only brought the bare essentials with me. It turned out that I visited their church on a Saturday afternoon, happened to meet their Pastor and I got invited to dance during Sunday's service. I felt totally "out of season" and not ready! Physically, I had been preparing for such a time as this, by working out everyday, but practically speaking, I had nothing (no music, costume, or even contact lenses!). My friends convinced me to stay one more night and said they'd "hook me up" with everything but the contacts. Not having any music on hand, I prayed while going through some CD's at the church. They had something with which I was familiar, and since it was on the top of the church's pile of music, I assumed they were very familiar with it as well.

I played the song once, kind of danced around the sanctuary (to get a 'feel' for the spacing) and felt like the Lord wanted me to dance to this particular one. Sunday morning came around and it was time to dance. I really had no idea what I was going to do, until I got up to the area and in the moments it took to get from my seat to the front, the Lord gave me a brief introductory outline. It was totally spontaneous or "on the spot." Everyone said it was anointed and some said they were crying. That always blesses me, when God does that.

Having a little bit of dance vocabulary helps, when you do something spontaneously. It is kind of like reading the Word. The more you read, the more comes out of you, when necessary. Likewise, the more dance that you practice, the more 'language' you have from which to draw. It is particularly helpful if you are trying to interpret something in front of people who are trying to understand what you are saying with your movements.

This brings me to the next point about the difference between songs that talk about God, songs of worship to God and prophetic ministry songs that come from God. I mentioned these earlier, briefly about where to direct your focus, however, here I'll talk a little more about what they are.

The songs that talk about God are ones that mention His character or attributes or what He does for us, etc. These make great presentation or dramatic type dances. Our focus could be toward the audience, or on an object, or kind of just straight ahead.

Worship songs are those of love or adoration directed toward our King. These are typically words, put to music, that attempt to adequately describe an indescribable love to an awesome God.

Finally, prophetic ministry songs or music come straight from the throne room and the very heart of the Father. In these songs, He is directing his love, adoration, life's directions, toward us. They are usually sung in first person as if God Himself were in the room talking directly to us. It sounds that way because

He is (through the song). Then visually, as a prophetic dancer, we can express the Father's heart, through movement.

In the dance I did, that particular Sunday, there were all three types of movement, as if it were three different songs. Typically speaking, though, a song or dance is either one or the other kind. Depicting a song three different ways, while it is playing through, one time, has taken several years of practice to accomplish, but it can be done (especially if you have the right song).

I started out with worship movements that were directed toward God. They were obvious words of adoration and love to which I did the appropriate 'reaching-to-heaven' type movements and spins.

In some parts of the song, it talked about the daily bread (the Word), so I quickly found a bible, on the pulpit and incorporated it into the dance. This, of course, was the segment talking about God. So, the movements were neither up nor down, but directed toward the object and gazing neutrally.

Finally, the last part of the song, even though the words were "I am desperate for you" (indicating, of course, our need for God), I turned it around to indicate to the people His desire for our love. At this point, I directed my focus toward the people as if God were talking right to them. I paused at a few individuals, as God lead, but generally, reached toward the entire congregation and looked into as many eyes, directly, as possible. Of course, this works ideally with prophetic music (which is almost all I like to dance to, these days). Under the circumstances, however, this is what the Lord provided. To minister to the hearts of that congregation, He gave me the "on the spot" directions, specifically for them.

There is something to watch for here. Prophetic dance has recently become very popular and with that, are movements done out in the audience (toward the people). What I've been starting to see lately, is that dancers are (out of a pure heart) going out into the audience to minister, because they've seen it done before (with results). The problem is, though, that often it is done by copying, not mirroring. <u>When we look into God's face and hear His voice, we reflect Him and His direction</u>. If we follow a person, and their direction (even if it is mine, from this book), then the results are less sure.

For example: If a song is talking about sending the latter rain, it really isn't appropriate to motion toward someone as if God is speaking to them. Though a dancer may have seen someone dance in front of someone before, if it is not God directed, with a God inspired, appropriate song, it will fall flat (with no anointing). The point is to listen to the words of the song and do appropriate movements at the appropriate time. You want your audience to not only understand what you are saying with your movements, but you also want ministry to come forth.

Conversely, however, if the words to the song were saying,

> *"You are my child and I have caught your tears, I want to calm your fears, today. Come into my arms, free from harm, I want to comfort you today.*
>
> *I've mended scars and healed your heart, I've walked you through before. So come to me my child, be free my child, let me comfort you today. I have not forgotten you my dear, I have known of all your dreams. I've not left you here, I'm with you my dear, let me wipe your tears away."*

The Lord is giving me these words, as I type, so I hope they bless you. At any rate, these type of words would be VERY appropriate with which to minister toward and in front of an individual.

To practice this kind of ministry, here are a few exercises that you can do with your team or at a workshop.

Ministering to a Congregation

This exercise is practice for an individual to minister to a congregation or group. Similar to a prophetic word coming forth in the congregation, so can a dancer interpret. I have done this through prophetic song as well as a spoken prophesy. It takes a little bit of practice (or some really good monitor speakers) to be able to hear what the prophet is saying and interpret instantly. There have been times, when I've actually been a second or two ahead of the minister. In other words, the Lord gave me the movement just before the prophet spoke. The reason that these exercises are so good to do, is so you can be ready at a moment's notice. It is like going to the gym and working with weights. You build strength and then increase the weight. Likewise, it is good to exercise your 'spiritual muscles', so when the weight of the prophetic anointing is evident, you have the spiritual strength with which to execute an excellent interpretation.

As I explain this next exercise, keep in mind that it is only an exercise. In other words, just like you would never hear several prophets giving a different word all at the same time, you would never have ten dancers interpreting one prophetic word ten different ways. That would be confusion! Remember, this is just practice.

Begin by splitting the group in half, each on respective sides of the room. Place an imaginary line down the center. Do not cross the line, as that is an imaginary edge of a ten foot high stage. The people on one half of the room sit, while the other half ministers a prophetic song to them.

The challenge is that (hopefully) the words to the song are unfamiliar and must be interpreted on the spot. Pick one person at a time (from across the room) at whom to gaze and then try to look at everyone at once, by panning. Play a portion of the song or the entire thing, then switch groups.

Remember, of course, to pick a song where God is talking in first person. Also, remember to look toward the audience as if God is talking *through* you. Therefore, your motions will be toward the people and not like a worship, toward God.

Change Awareness

Sometimes, the Lord will want you to minister to one individual for a minute and then switch to someone else, for the rest of the song or word. In these next exercises, you can practice that.

Make two large concentric circles (inside and outside). First, the outside circle will minister to the inside. Make sure that there is an even number, so that there is a one to one ratio.

When the music begins, the people on the outside of the circle interpret toward the person in front of them. I usually say, here not to touch, speak to, or pray for the other person. Only let the words of the prophetic music and the movement interpretation do the ministry.

After about a minute, the outside circle rotates clockwise, putting them in front of a new person. Do this about three or four times, so that people get to receive from different individuals.

An alternative to this exact same method would be to have the inside circle minister to the outside by having the outside circle sit on the floor (or in chairs). You could even have the inside circle sit down. The actual position doesn't really matter. It is the practice that does.

Let's say the inside circle just received ministry. Now, they can be the ministers. Have the previous outside circle go sit in the front rows and down the aisles either of your actual sanctuary or an imaginary one (depending on where you have practice). Then the new ministers randomly choose to whom they minister. The leader or moderator would then say 'switch', after which everyone finds a new person to whom they minister. Like the circles, do this about three or four times. Have the Kleenex boxes near by. People always receive from the Lord and their hearts get touched, through song or word.

Challenge

Get in small groups of five or six. Let one person get in the center of the circle. Each person on the outside takes turns prophesying to the person in the center, switching quickly and rotating counter clockwise. Go two times around the circle, then let the next person get in the center. This can be done with either prophetic music with words, where all the dancer has to do is interpret the words. However, for a real challenge, have only prophetic music, with no words and have the dancers give a quick word with their movement. As each person gives their word, it is like a puzzle and when everyone is finished, the central person has a complete picture of what God is saying to them.

Ministering prophetically, on the spot, can be challenging, but worthwhile. After practicing a little, you feel more comfortable with allowing the Lord to work through you and then watching the amazing results of ministry. When you see the transformation on someone's face or see the visible change that has taken place, it is so incredible. Ultimately, to see someone set free through prophetic dance, is delightful to our Lord!

Chapter Five
PRE-PLANNED?

Even a choreographed dance that has not only been divinely inspired by God and prayed through, but also danced under the anointing of Holy Spirit can be considered prophetic. This type of dance should portray the gospel message, and minister God's anointing in order to break the yoke of bondage, and set the captives free. Through the dance, we are calling those things into existence that be not as though they were. We can speak the Word, make declarations, and prophesy God's will even through planned movements.

Most often, when we say 'prophetic dance', we think of spontaneous movement. However, we don't need to get stuck there. So many times, over the years, while in my prayer closet, the Lord would specifically give me choreography to a certain song. It was always the song of the hour with a message of the day. Therefore, since it was inspired of God and is a message from God, then it could possibly be a prophetic word.

If we are speaking those things into existence that be not as though they were, then the audience is seeing and hearing something that never was and are receiving a message that now is. This may sound like a play on words, but think of the ministerial results. A song, coupled with a visual message, is powerful enough to touch even the hardest heart. Isn't this our goal as dancers anyway? After all, we are called to be ministers of the gospel, using dance is our medium. It is not the reverse. We are not called to be dancers using ministry as our tool to perform.

This is kind of a fine line, though and we as dancers must be especially careful to mind our heart motivation. It is true, that we do perform (in a sense) by virtue of being in front of people who watch us with their eyes open. The Pastor would never announce: "...and now the dance team will present a ministry dance. Will you please close your eyes." That is absurd! An audience must see a dance to receive what God has to say through its message. <u>So, we dancers, in a divinely inspired piece, must be sure we are presenting it with clean hands and a pure heart</u>.

<u>It is all about the heart</u>. Like the worship leader, who is presenting God's heart to the people during praise and worship, so must a dancer present and represent God's heart during a choreographed dance. This would make

it prophetic because it is a divinely inspired utterance, presented through a dancer's language of movement. If our motivation is to be seen or to perform, it will come across as just that and ministry will not take place.

There are many, many examples of when choreographed dances have touched the hearts of the congregation. In my experience, there has been one particular instance that has had the most dramatic results. While in my prayer time, the Lord showed me a dance and let me know that people would respond. He showed me that, at the end of the dance, we were to carry five yard gold lame cloths (representing the glory of God) over the congregation. Both times we did the dance, people fell out under the power of the Holy Ghost, right there in the pews! One time we did it, the people in the congregation were weeping and repenting, and afterward came to the alter area for ministry. The anointing was so strong that people were literally crawling to the alter.

As the years went on, and I did more and more solo dancing, I kind of got away from choreographing. I enjoyed using prophetic music, and dancing to it spontaneously, instead. However, this one particular time, the Lord wanted me to actually choreograph a dance to a prophetic song. Remember, when I refer to prophetic music, I mean the kind where God talks directly, in first person.

This dance was designed for a friend's wedding. The Lord showed me to act out the first part of the dance as if He were talking to me and I was the recipient of His word. Then, in the second part of the dance, I was representing God and ministered the rest of the song outward, looking directly to various people. He had me look at first, toward the bride and groom, then the bridesmaids and groomsmen, their immediate family, and finally all the guests (as I exited down the aisle). The results were that it touched hearts. Many people came to me afterwards and said that during the dance, they were crying and it blessed them tremendously.

We've been talking a little bit about presentation pieces, as prophetic dance. Now, I'd like to talk about choreographed prophetic dance, done during praise and worship. Again, this may seem like a contradiction of terms—choreographed and prophetic. However, that is if we only think of prophetic dance as spontaneous.

There is something that I have coined as 'planned spontaneity', again which seems like a contradiction it terms, but is a practical combination and application of both choreographed, and prophetic dance. This term is also in my Creative Worship book, but bares repetition in this context.

You can choreograph something to a worship song, in the very short period of time, right before praise and worship. You can 'plan' for certain people to do certain parts. You can 'plan' to use certain props. You can 'plan' for certain times of entrance and exit. You can 'plan' for certain types of movements to be done during certain times in the song. On the other hand, you can spontaneously do the movements with those props. You can spontaneously lead the rest of the team through movements, during that certain time of entrance or exit. You can spontaneously create movement during the chorus, when everyone is supposed to be in a certain place. Does this make sense? It is planning some parts and filling in the rest with spontaneity. It works extremely well, especially if you don't have much time, before you know what the worship songs are going to be (for that particular service).

People can work on this type of activity during dance team practice time. Here are some exercises.

Planned Spontaneity

Simply break up into groups of about four or five. Pick a particular song that would be easy to interpret and that could be divided up into parts. Have the groups take about three minutes to talk about who would do what part and what would be done spontaneously. For example: if the song says something like, "let the wind blow, let the glory come, let the fire fall, let the river flow…" the group might do some quick part picking. One person could represent the wind, one the glory, one the fire, and one the river. This would be easy as props, with the appropriate colors could be incorporated. Perhaps, when each hears their part in the song, they could do something spontaneous to that. While the others do something quietly in the background. Then during the verses, perhaps another person could dance a solo, without props. That only took about thirty seconds!

Sometimes, we would dance (kind of follow the leader) spontaneously to a certain worship song and by the end of that song, had some movements that really worked. What would end up happening was that it became choreographed, by virtue of spontaneous experimentation. Nevertheless, it was still God inspired, because it was done under the anointing, by vessels who allowed themselves to be openly used by Him.

Half and Half

Another exercise: Once you've gotten some basic movements to a particular song, practice that, during your practice times. For instance, you may want to have the chorus always choreographed a certain way, but have different people lead each verse, spontaneously, and have the others follow.

Whether a dance is totally choreographed and presented in front of a congregation, or partially choreographed and partially spontaneous, or done with planned spontaneity, they can all be prophetic. They can all speak those things into existence that be not as though they were. The can all be divinely inspired utterances, spoken through a dancers language of love. They can all minister to the onlooker's heart, which should be our goal.

Chapter Six
POWER OF PRAISE

Just like we have warfare praise songs, there is also warfare dance. This can be actual movements that look like we are tearing down strongholds, or stomping on the enemy, etc.; or it could be a choreographed piece depicting warfare. However, the mere fact that we are Spirit filled vessels praising the Lord through dance, sets the enemy to flight! Psalm 8:2 says: "Out of the mouth of babes…You have ordained strength (interpreted as praise), because of your enemies, that You may silence (diminish) the enemy and the avenger." Basically, God has ordained praise so we may make the enemy get smaller and finally disappear. Again, when God inhabits the praises of His people and we praise Him through the dance, then He inhabits us and the enemy must go! This is another reason why it is important to dance during praise and worship. We are prophesying the Word of the Lord, through our bodies, tearing down strongholds, diminishing the enemy of our souls, and preparing the spiritual atmosphere, so people may receive what the Lord has for them, and that they might gain freedom. As you read ahead to the scriptural references provided in this chapter, you will discover that many of the motions we do are not just pretty gestures, but actual prophetic demonstrations of God's awesome, foe-defeating power.

When this discovery became a revelation, it transformed my dancing (or at least my understanding of the dance). I began to research the various words and then the Lord wanted me to put them all together in one book. Now, all thirty-one Hebrew, English, and Greek words, pertaining to dance or movement (along with their associated scriptures) are in the Dance, Dance, Dance! book.

During workshops, I began incorporating exercises that utilized these words, as well as other scriptures, so that learning the scriptures would be fun and easy.

How much more prophetic can we get? When depicting the very Word of God, from the Bible, you can't go wrong. These are certainly pure words from God.

The following exercises; Word Interpretation and Psalm 91, do not have to remain within the four walls of the practice room or conference center. These exercises could be practiced and then presented as an illustrated sermon. They could also be a prelude or enhancement to the message, if the dance team were aware of what passage of scripture the Pastor was going to use, that particular day.

I just happen to have chosen these particular words and scriptures because they are familiar to most people and easy to depict. Feel free to copy the pages from this text to hand out to people like scripts, so you may practice. If you would like more copies of this book or the Dance, Dance, Dance! book, please see the end of this book for contact information.

Active Word Study

Use the "PRAISE" pages (below) and divide the team into six groups.

One person, in each group, becomes the designated reader. You may want to switch around, so the reader can see the creation also.

The rest of group makes a dance/drama to the associated scripture (using body sculpting and design shapes).

While practicing your scriptural interpretation, and you come across the bold, italicized word, in that scripture, be sure to interpret that using one of the definitions associated with that word. For example: When the reader comes to the word ***leaping*** in the scripture, the rest of the team (or whomever they decided is supposed to depict that word) would do what the definition is.

The bold, italicized words (right next to the Hebrew, Greek, or English words) are simply 'locator words'. These help you find the word, in the scripture, that is being defined.

When it comes time to present, the reader will read the word and definition. They can also tell what is the italicized word, in the scripture, and which definition the group chose to use.

As the reader, then reads the scripture, the rest of the team enacts *only* the scripture. There is no need to act out the definition (unless that is your preference).

The following is just a small sample of the thirty-one words. After doing this exercise, with such success (during the workshops), we then expanded. Over a two day workshop, we attempted to depict all of the scriptures and learn all of their associated words. This evolved into the 'Active Word Study', which has become a standard exercise (as well as a requested favorite) in the workshops.

P-R-A-I-S-E

P—*Pazaz* – *(Made strong; Leaping)* To spring as if separating the limbs, like leaping; to bound; to be light and agile.

II Samuel 6:16 – And as the ark of the Lord came into the city of David, Michal, Saul's daughter looked through a window, and saw king David **leaping** and dancing before the Lord; and she despised him in her heart.

R—*Raqad or Rekad*—**(Dance; Skip; Leap; Jump; Worship)** To stamp; spring about wildly for joy; dance; jump; leap; skip.

Ecclesiastes 3:4 – A time to weep, and a time to laugh; a time to mourn, and a time to **dance**.

A—*Agalliao*—**(Rejoice; Leap; Gladness; Joy)** (From original Greek—Agallo—"very much leaping") Jump for joy; exult; leap up; be exceedingly glad or joyful; to make glorious; exalt; rejoice greatly.

Acts 2:46—And they, continuing daily with one accord in the temple, and breaking bread from house to house, did eat their meat with **gladness** and singleness of heart.

I—I will Rejoice (this makes the acronym work) *Gil, Giyl, Gul, or Guwl* (pronounced gool or geel) - **(Rejoice; Be joyful)** To spin around under the influence of any violent emotion (usually of joy or rejoicing; to go in a circle; to be glad; joy; be joyful; rejoice; cry out; exalt.

Psalm 48:11—Let mount Zion **rejoice**, let the daughters of Judah be glad, because of thy judgments.

S—*Skirtao*—**(Leap)** To jump; move; leap for joy.

Luke 6:23—Rejoice ye in that day, and **leap for joy**: for, behold, your reward is great in heaven; for in the like manner did their fathers unto the prophets.

E—*Elats or Ealaz*—*(Triumph; Go up; Rejoice)* To jump for joy; exult [root—salient—jumping; leaping; gushing or jetting forth; standing out from the rest; noticeable; conspicuous; prominent; the part of a battle line, trench, fort, etc. which projects farthest toward the enemy (to rejoice greatly; be jubilant; glory; to leap up; leap for joy; triumphant)].

Psalm 25:2—O my God, I trust in thee: let me not be ashamed, let not mine enemies ***triumph*** over me.

Movement Through The Word

This exercise could be done with any scripture, but I've just written this portion of Psalm 91 for easy reference. It is nicely done in a semi-circle (perhaps around the front of the sanctuary), where the various groups present their verse sequentially.

First divide the group up according to the number of verses that need to be read. Then, practice with a skit, drama, movements, shapes or designs that would depict that particular verse. Once the groups have rehearsed enough, and are ready to present, one person should read, slowly and dramatically.

The transitions between verses may need a little practice, so the following group knows when the previous' group is finished. This is important to practice so the whole scripture may be read with continuity.

Once the whole scripture (or at least the chosen section) has been read, then the entire group may want to end with something cohesive, like a group shape. Another idea may be to go right into a dance afterward. Be sure to practice your exit as well.

For this example, divide into seven groups to interpret a portion of Psalm 91. Feel free to make copies of the next page, for ease with practice. Whenever we did this, during workshops, there was always a powerful anointing and people were extremely blessed.

God's word is life. It is wonderful to bring that life to light through prophetic acts of dance or drama.

Psalm 91

"He who dwells in the secret place of the Most High, shall abide under the shadow of the Almighty.

I will say of the Lord, He is my refuge and my fortress; my god, in Him I will trust.

Surely, He shall deliver you from the snare of the fowler and from the perilous pestilence.

He shall cover you with His feathers, and under

His wings, you shall take refuge; His truth shall be your shield and buckler.

You shall not be afraid of terror by night, nor of the arrow that flies by day

Nor of the pestilence that walks in darkness, nor of the destruction that lays waste at noonday.

A thousand may fall at your side, and ten thousand at your right hand; but it shall not come near you."[2]

Chapter Seven
HEALED!

Often, when someone is sick and in need of healing, their faith needs to be stirred. It needs to be 'activated' (like active dry yeast). Yeast will not bubble, fizz, or do what it is supposed to, until it is activated by coming in contact with an activating substance—water. Likewise, people who need healing, sometimes need their faith activated through a point of contact between the natural and supernatural.

Acts 5:15-16—*"So that they brought the sick out into the streets and laid them on beds and couches, that at least the shadow of Peter passing by might fall on some of them. Vs. 16 Also a multitude gathered from the surrounding cities to Jerusalem, bringing sick people and those who were tormented by unclean spirits, and they were all healed."*[2]

See also: Luke 8:44,48; Matthew 14:35-36; Matthew 20:30; & John 9:1 & 7

Even as Peter's shadow healed the sick, so can healing and deliverance come forth through a yielded, moving, glory-filled vessel. We, as prophetic dancers, can be a point of contact for faith activation.

It always amazes me, when we do prophetic exercises, how many healings and deliverances take place. Ever so gently, does Holy Spirit work.

I'll never forget one time when I was ministering in a very small church and they wanted me to dance during the Sunday service. The Lord led me to a song about intercession where in the middle, there is wonderful prophetic instrumental music (with an emphasis on the violin). I always ministered this dance spontaneously, allowing the Lord to lead me. I started on the platform and stayed there during all the words of the song. When it began to go into the prophetic instrumental part, I came down on the floor, so I could go out into the congregation.

While spinning in front of the first row, on the left, they watched and received. I then, spun around in front of the people on the right. When I happened to look back to the left, I noticed that the people in the front row had fallen over in their laps and were weeping. As I began proceeding down the aisle, not only did I notice the people on the right had also fallen over, but there were whispering sounds of tears throughout the congregation. It reminded me of that scripture about Peter's shadow 'passing by' and the people were healed.

One meeting, during the prophetic dance portion of the workshop, the Lord wanted me to ask if there was anyone there who was sick or in pain. Six people raised their hands, so I asked them to come up front and stand in two lines. We prayed, and I asked the Lord for direction and for His healing virtue to flow. I then danced around them, individually, weaving in and among them. Some began to weep. Others, I stood behind and did some movements indicating that bonds would be removed from their wrists and ankles; that a band of pressure, from around their head would be lifted. I motioned that the burdens that they were carrying (on their shoulders) were heavy, as I removed them and replaced them with God's light burden. Some people, I went around toward their stomachs and motioned to 'pull out' their infirmity or oppression. It was a very intense spiritual encounter with the Almighty.

Afterwards, I listened to their testimonies and heard that one woman had been sitting down, during the morning session, because her back hurt so badly. She said that after I danced around her, that her back pain was gone! She was able to complete the rest of the afternoon's activities. Another woman said that she had a terrible headache and after I motioned to remove the 'pressure band' off of her head, she said it was gone. We gave God all the praise!

There was one time when a mother had brought her troubled teen with her to practice. Earlier in the day, the Lord had told me that we were all to pray for each other just before practice (before we actually started dancing). I noticed that this one mom was having a little trouble with her daughter, so I went over to see if I could help. I immediately saw a demonic oppression on her and began to dance. I remembered the word Cabab, a Hebrew word which means to revolve, surround or border; to walk; whirl. I also remembered one of my favorite scriptures: *Psalm 32: 7—"Thou art my hiding place; thou shalt preserve me from trouble; thou shat compass (Cabab) me about with songs of deliverance."*[2] So, I proceeded to do the Word. I danced around her. Then I remembered the word Karar, another Hebrew word which means to dance or whirl; to go around in a circle. This comes from the root word kar, which means battering ram. Therefore, it could be like a battering ram whirling against the enemy! I saw the young girl feeling a little bit uncomfortable, so I spun, dramatically, three times in front of her. After each spin, I directed my sharply extended arm toward her belly. After the third spin, there was a breakthrough! We saw a noticeably different look on her countenance. She had been delivered. Then we practiced our dances unfettered.

Healing and Deliverance

There are countless stories of God's goodness and healing virtue that has flowed through the dance. However, I want to share some exercises with you, to help you practice this.

The following are some 'activations' that probably should be done in a supervised setting. It may be a good idea to have a Pastor or Elder with your group, when these are done, for good spiritual oversight. On one hand, we want to feel at ease (and we should). However, on the other hand, we must also realize the awesome responsibility and potential to change lives is there. As we allow the all powerful God to use our physical bodies to enact or visually demonstrate what He is saying or doing, He is thereby revealing Himself to us and then through us. Also, physical, mental, and emotional healing, can take place when we allow His movements to flow through us. God's healing virtue and delivering power are released in the earth realm when our bodies are submitted, willingly as His extension from the spirit realm.

Often, the exercise depends on the song. One workshop, we had a song that talked about people looking in the mirror and discovering what they saw. It was about how they viewed themselves. The very next song was a response from God to those looking in the mirror. He was pouring out His love and adoration to the onlooker and saying how much beauty that He saw.

I had the group get into two concentric circles (one inside the other), where the inside circle faced the outside. The outside circle played the part of God and basically watched while the inside group depicted how they felt. There were some other motions, that I gave them that went with the music, too. Then it was God's turn to respond. When the inside group heard His words and saw their motions, there was some healing.

Later, I took the inside circle and made them a different type of outside circle. With a different prophetic song, they then became the ministers. The people who played the part of God previously, now, one at a time got into the center of the circle. Who ever felt lead would take turns ministering to that individual. So, there was a fairly large outside circle, with one individual receiving ministry from one other individual.

Meanwhile, the outside circle was moving slowly around those two, representing the Father's arms of comfort. As they compassed with songs of deliverance, the person in the middle received ministry. As Holy Spirit lead, either other people would take turns ministering to that individual, or another person would get in the center. It just flowed.

Many times I've done a dance that speaks of coming to the still waters, lying in the green pastures, and walking with the Lord in His garden. Every single time, with out fail, people really receive ministry. Some tear up, some weep through their healing, and some wail through their deliverance. What ever the response, the evidence proves God ministers healing through the dance.

Word of Knowledge

When the Lord showed me this exercise, I was a bit apprehensive, as I had not done it much at all, myself. With an obedient heart, I taught about ministering to someone after receiving a word of knowledge. Jesus said, "My words are spirit and they are life." When we know this, we should be able to speak the truth and speak life, if we speak His Words.

In this particular exercise, get in a large circle and pray specifically to see if you can see, hear, or sense an infirmity. For example: ask the Lord to show you if someone, in the circle, has some kind of an ailment (like back pain, earache, arthritis, etc.).

Someone should then volunteer what they think they got. Be reminded (if you are going to try this with your group, that it is only practice and you can't go wrong by trying). Once it is spoken out, then if someone in the circle (or even a relative of someone in the circle) has that particular ailment, then they should come to the center for healing.

On a side note, here, I was at a prophetic training session and did this exercise with a group. Someone had called out that they sensed arthritis. At that time, my right middle knuckle was experiencing some pain. In fact, for a couple of weeks, I could not open jars or lift plates, because of the pain. So, I jumped right in the center of the circle. The person who had called it out with trepidation, prayed specifically for me, while the others in the circle prayed from their distance. The next day, I was totally healed and have been ever since!

I was so excited about that and was especially excited when the Lord showed me that this same thing could be done through dance.

So, instead of the person who called it out coming up and just praying for the person whose ailment it was, that person would dance around them for healing. In one case, I had them pray out loud for the person, as they did dance moves, and the results were amazing. People really did hear from God for the others in the circle and people did receive healing when we danced and prayed.

God is so good and desires that we prosper and be in good health. It is not his desire that we are sick, but healed. He is Jehovah Rophe, the Lord

God our healer. By His stripes we are healed. Let the balm of Gilead pour over you from the top of your head to the souls of your feet, like a warm soothing oil of anointing. Allow the God of the dance, to dance over you with joy and through a vessel of praise. Be that vessel to prophetically release a healing anointing toward the hurting and afflicted. Enjoy being that vessel of healing as well as being healed by the Almighty.

Heart hearts - locked in help is blocked out
remove block & barriers

Conclusion

Whether you are a seasoned prophet or are just getting your feet wet, as a born again believer, you can stir up that gift within you.

You can use movement accompanied by music and/or words. You can use your voice accompanied with or without movement. Either way, you can minister for the Creator of the Universe.

It is my hope and desire that you will be 'activated' to use that resident gift of prophesy so God may heal, deliver, and set the captive free.

The important thing is that those who are called are called to minister and not perform. We are called to preach the gospel, by whatever means God provides, such as word, song, or dance. Hopefully, I shed some light on the means of various forms of prophetic dance, so you may lovingly and exuberantly, *express the Father's heart*.

MUSIC SUGGESTIONS

The following is a list of, either artists or locations from where good prophetic music may be found.

- elijahlist.com
- kimclement.com
- Joann Mcfatter's music *(found on elijahlist.com)*
- Jasonupton.com
- Kimberly & Alberto Rivera *(found on elijahlist.com)*
- Donald Lawrence *Go Get Your Life Back CD* Song "Seasons" *(found in gospel bookstores)*

Lynn M. Hayden

BIBLIOGRAPHY

---

[1] *The Exhaustive Concordance of the Bible*
Abingdon Press, Nashville Forty-second Printing 1983
James Strong Madison, N.J.
Key Word Comparison © 1980 by Abingdon

[2] *Spirit Filled Life Bible – New King James Version*
Scripture quotations and some comments
Thomas Nelson Publishers – Nashville – Atlanta – London – Vancouver
Thomas Nelson, Inc. ©1991
General Editor – Jack W. Hayford, Litt. D.
Old Testament Editor – Sam Middlebrook, D. Min.
New Testament Editor – Jerry Horner, Th.D.
Assistant Editor – Gary Mastdorf, M.S.

[3] *Webster's New World Dictionary of the American Language*
Simon and Schuster, a division of Gulf and Western Corp. ©1982
1230 Avenue of the Americas
New York, New York 10020

[4] *The American Heritage Dictionary of the English Language*
© 1969,1970 American Heritage Publishing Co., Inc.
551 Fifth Avenue, New York, New York 10017

William Morris, Editor

CONTACT INFORMATION

Dancing For Him Ministries, Inc.

If you would like to host a *PROPHETIC DANCE WORKSHOP,* or further information about general conferences, speaking engagements, DVD's, and ordering more books, please feel free to visit **www.dancingforhim.com.**

bridal veil
" cord
crown
sword